PIG
Parade

"I don't think I will ever get tired of wearing **pink.**" —Emma Bunton

PIGGY PARADE

"THE NOSE SCENTS AND IT CHOOSES. AN ARTIST IS SIMPLY A KIND OF PIG SNOUTING TRUFFLES."

–Igor Stravinsky

It all started in a pigsty. Then came the Big Bad Wolf, the dictatorial pigs of Orwell's *Animal Farm,* and Babe the courageous little pig on the big screen. However, fame has not gone to the pig's head and he is still humble, sociable, intelligent and, contrary to what you would expect, clean. Yes, because rolling in the mud is just a way of keeping your skin free of parasites.

Although there are numerous breeds of pig, of different size, color and appearance, the pig we all know and love is pink, with pointed ears and a characteristic flat nose. And above all, he is always rummaging in search of food, combing every available inch of ground without stopping. The pig's bristly hairs and little curly tail inspire immediate affection in observers. When pigs interact with each other or when they are in the company of other animals, pigs adopt airs which are amusing, to say the least. But they are sweet and adorable when they lie stretched out on the ground, as those who have chosen a pig as a pet well know.

WHO'S AFRAID OF THE BIG, BAD WOLF?

BOW AND SCRAPE

"To be yourself in a world that is constantly trying to make you something else is the greatest accomplishment."

—Ralph Waldo Emerson

BREAKFAST AT TIFFANY'S

"I am a slow walker, but I never walk backwards."

–Abraham Lincoln

THREE LITTLE PIGS

ESKIMO KISS

"I like the word 'indolence'...

It makes my laziness seem classy." –Bern Williams

SQUABBLE

"Listen to many, speak to a few."

–William Shakespeare

"Continual cheerfulness is a sign of wisdom."

–Irish proverb

"Butterflies are always following me, everywhere I go."

—Mariah Carey

ESCAPE ATTEMPT

"Concern should drive us into action,

not into depression."   –Karen Horney

–William Paley

"Who can refute a sneer?"

DUET

"Normal is nothing more than a cycle on a washing machine."

–Whoopi Goldberg

"I've been on a diet for two weeks
and all I've lost is fourteen days."

–Totie Fields

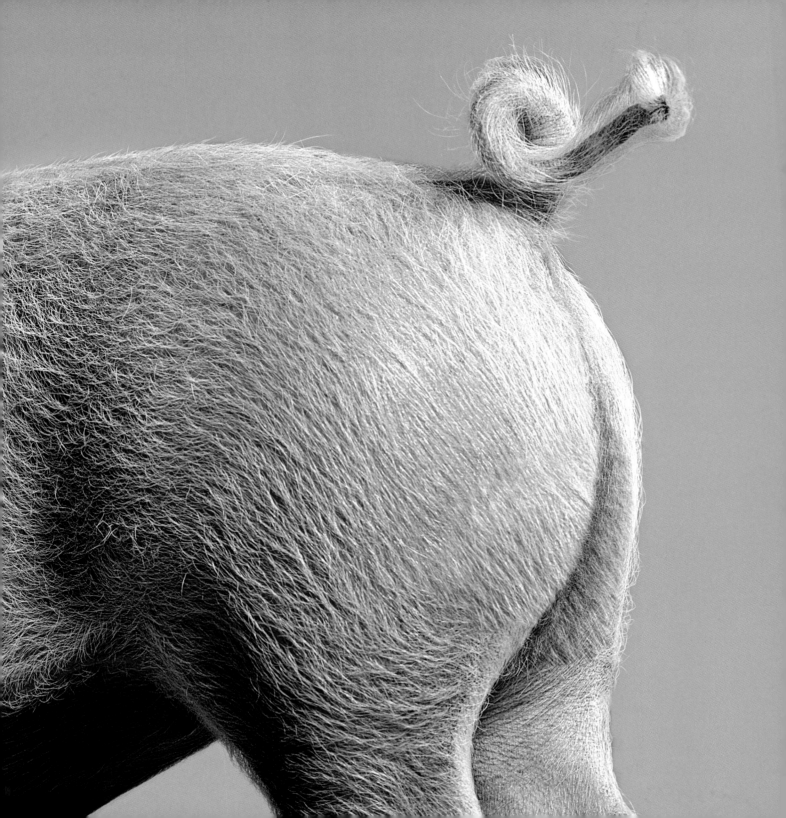

"All that's left is some pink paint from the pig."

—Robert Garrison

"I CAN'T GET NO SATISFACTION."

–Rolling Stones

48

"He who tip-toes cannot stand; he who strides cannot walk."

—Jean de la Bruyère

"Pigs are playful. Pigs are pink. Pigs are smarter than you think."

–Charles Ghigna

"I fell off my **PINK** cloud with a thud." —Elizabeth Taylor

"Young pigs grunt as old pigs grunted before them."

—Danish proverb

"Life is a series of commas, not periods. " –Matthew McConaughey

—Erma Bombeck

"If you can't make it better, you can laugh at it."

"We're all in the same pool."

–Stacy Hephner

"It's hard to be funny when you have to be clean."

–Mae West

BEAUTY FARM

"The coward threatens when he is safe." –Johann Wolfgang von Goethe

"It takes two to get one in trouble."   –Mae West

"The most called-upon prerequisite
of a friend is an accessible ear."

–Maya Angelou

"This life is not for complaint,
but for satisfaction."

–Henry David Thoreau

ENTRY ON THE SCENE

"If you can find a path with no obstacles, it probably doesn't lead anywhere."

—Frank A. Clark

"In every society some men are born to rule,
and some to advise."

–Ralph Waldo Emerson

IMPOSSIBLE LOVE

"I love sleep. My life has the tendency to fall apart when I'm awake."

—Ernest Hemingway

"A pig used to dirt turns its nose up at rice."

–Japanese proverb

„Give every man thy ear, but few thy voice."

— *William Shakespeare*

MOUSE...

...PIG

ORIGINAL SIN

THE GREAT ESCAPE

"Sometimes the most urgent thing you can possibly do...

is take a complete rest." —Ashleigh Brilliant

"I find nothing more depressing than optimism."

—Paul Fussell

"I like boring things."

–Andy Warhol

"Long engagements
give people the opportunity of finding out
each other's character before marriage,
which is never advisable."

–Oscar Wilde

ATTENTIVE

INATTENTIVE

"I only ask to be free. The butterflies are free."

–Charles Dickens

PHOTO FINISH

"Smell is a potent wizard that transports you across thousands of miles and all the years you have lived."

–Helen Keller

"It is better to keep your mouth shut and appear
stupid than to open it and remove all doubt."

–Mark Twain

"Little pig, little pig, let me come in!" "Not by the hair on my chinny-chin-chin!" "Then I'll huff, and I'll puff, and I'll blow your house in."

–Three Little Pigs

"Once upon a time when pigs spoke rhyme and monkeys chewed tobacco..."

–The Three Little Pigs

"We may look mild, but we're wild."

—Bruce Sherman

COUNTRY STYLE

"Perplexity is the beginning of knowledge."

–Khalil Gibran

WILD INSTINCT